W9-AWN-287

VICTORY
IN THE GULF

DEDICATED TO THE FIGHTING
MEN AND WOMEN
OF DESERT STORM

COLLECTOR'S EDITION

PUBLICATIONS INTERNATIONAL, LTD.

Copyright © 1991 Publications International, Ltd. All rights reserved. This book may not be reproduced or quoted in whole or in part by mimeograph or any other printed or electronic means, or for presentation on radio, television, videotape, or film without written permission from:
Louis Weber, C.E.O.
Publications International, Ltd.
7373 North Cicero Avenue
Lincolnwood, Illinois 60646

Permission is never granted for commercial purposes.

Manufactured in U.S.A.

8 7 6 5 4 3 2 1

TABLE OF CONTENTS

An F-14 Tomcat takes off from the USS *Constellation*.

M-1 Abrams MBTs.

Marines with 60mm mortar.

Destroyed APC from the Battle of Khafji.

INTRODUCTION: STORMING TO VICTORY

To understand the Persian Gulf War, it is necessary to understand the past. The Gulf War was not the first major conflict in the Middle East, nor is it likely to be the last. The Mideast has been torn by strife for centuries, reaching as far back as the time of the Crusades and earlier. As the birthplace of Judaism, Christianity, and Islam, religion has always played a major role in the strife of this land. In the 20th century, oil thrust the Middle East onto the world stage.

The next few pages detail some of the more important events of the recent past affecting the Mideast today: previous U.S. involvement in the Mideast, the founding of Israel, the tragic civil war in Lebanon, and the Iran-Iraq War—an eight-year war that toughened Iraqi troops to the rigors of desert warfare. Desert Shield was a five-month period in which Allied nations built up their armed forces to face Saddam Hussein's army. Then came Desert Storm, opening with a month-long air war against Iraqi troops and war-making capabilities. Finally, Allied forces—such as these U.S. soldiers of the 1st Battalion, 3rd Regiment—began the final phase, the land war. It was only a matter of time before victory was assured.

ABOVE: F-111 and FB-111 Aardvarks delivered a punishing blow to Libya in 1986 in retaliation for continued terrorist activity originating in that country.

ABOVE: Colonel Muammar Qaddafi — who came to power in 1969 — has been an adversary of the United States for decades.

ABOVE: The United States became militarily involved in the Lebanon civil war in the early 1980s. In October 1983, a suicide terrorist drove a vehicle filled with explosives into the command center of the U.S. Marines stationed in Beirut. More than 200 soldiers were killed.

PRELUDE TO WAR

U.S. INVOLVEMENT IN THE MIDEAST

The interests of the United States in the Mideast can be summed up in two words: Israel and oil. These interests conflict sharply. Israel is a strong ally and democratic outpost in this volatile region, but has no oil. Many other nations of the Mideast — Saudi Arabia and Kuwait, to name two — have huge reserves of oil, but they are sworn enemies of Israel. The antipathy of Israel and its Arab neighbors stems from religious differences. Israel is a predominately Jewish state; the Arab nations are predominately Islamic. To ensure peace, the United States must find a path between these two conflicting interests.

ABOVE: The existence of large quantities of oil in the Middle East—exemplified by this Kuwaiti oil refinery—has wielded great influence on America's involvement in the region. BELOW: One way the U.S. protects its interests in the Mideast is through military power. Here, an F-14 Tomcat takes off from an aircraft carrier. Tomcats tangled with Libyan jets twice in the 1980s.

ISRAEL, A HOME FOR THE JEWISH PEOPLE

From its founding in 1948, Israel has had to fight for its right to exist. Its Arab neighbors have tried several times—in 1948, 1956, 1967, and 1973—to obliterate this tiny nation. Why? Religious differences are the hallmark of the conflict between Israel and its neighbors. Israel is a sanctuary for the world's Jews; it is a home for any Jew who wishes to immigrate there. The Arabs believe this same land should belong to the Palestinians, an Arabic people without a nation of their own. The Islamic people—mostly Arabs— cannot tolerate a Jewish state on land they consider theirs. Control of the land around the Jordan River brings control of Jerusalem, a city sacred to Jews, Christians, and Muslims.

Golda Meir was one of the founders of Israel. She also served as her nation's fourth prime minister, from 1969 to 1974.

Soldier and statesman Moshe Dayan led Israel to victory during the 1967 Six-Day War. His greatest influence over Israel's foreign affairs came in the early 1970s.

ABOVE: Any peace for Israel almost surely will involve Yasser Arafat, leader of the Palestine Liberation Organization.

RIGHT: In 1978, an historic peace agreement, brokered by President Jimmy Carter, was signed by Egypt's Anwar Sadat and Israel's Menachem Begin. The peace settlement ended the conflict between Israel and Egypt but had little effect on Israel's relations with other Arab nations.

ABOVE: Egyptian armor and troops move into action against Israeli forces during the 1948 war.

BELOW: Israeli artillery pound Egyptian positions during the Six-Day War, 1967, opening the road to the Suez Canal.

ABOVE: Israeli infantry wait on the heights outside Kusseima, Egypt, before an attack on October 30, 1956.

BELOW: On Yom Kippur in 1973, several Arab nations attacked an unprepared Israel. Here, Israeli troops, riding atop armored personnel carriers, head toward the front.

LEBANON, CEDARS AND STRIFE

The Lebanon nation was formed by the fiat of France, a colonial power in the region. Originally, the nation was about half Christian and half Muslim, and the machinations of government recognized that split. Over the decades, that ratio changed, and the nation now has an overwhelming Islamic majority. However, the government structure was not altered to meet this change.

In the mid-1970s, civil war broke out between various religious factions, and fighting continues to this day. The chaos of the civil war afforded the PLO a base of operations for many years, until the Israelis drove them out in the early 1980s. Today, the misery of Lebanon reflects the misery of the Mideast— kidnappings, car bombs, militias, and various occupying forces, such as Israel and Syria.

ABOVE: **Christian militiamen fire on other Christian militia in East Beirut in early 1990.**

ABOVE: **The United Nations supplied a peacekeeping force in an attempt to quell Lebanon's violence. These Swedish troops in an armored personnel carrier patrol a street in Lebanon in 1988.**

RIGHT: **Lebanese citizens wounded during artillery duels between Christian militia troops and Syrian troops are evacuated to a French hospital ship.**

A GRUELING DESERT WAR

ABOVE: The Shah of Iran was deposed in 1979. He had been an ally of the U.S.

ABOVE: The Ayatollah Khomeini came to power after the Shah and turned Iran into a theocracy.

ABOVE: Iraqi troops celebrate during the Iran-Iraq War. At different times, each side advanced far into the other nation's territory, but the war was basically a stalemate.

During his reign, the Shah of Iran brought the technology and lifestyle of the West to Iran. Although this pleased many Iranians, many others—preferring a fundamentalist form of Islam—were distressed and angered by this development. After the Shah was deposed in 1979, Khomeini set up a government based on the religion of Islam. Iran became a fundamentalist Islamic state. The Iranian people rejected all Western influences, and the United States became the "Great Satan."

In September 1980, Iraqi President Saddam Hussein invaded Iran, hoping to take advantage of the chaos in Iran following the overthrow of the Shah. Hussein miscalculated. Iran fought back with thousands of religious fanatics willing to die for Allah. The United States and many Arab nations supported Iraq because of their fear of the Islamic fanaticism of Iran. The United States provided protection to noncombatant shipping during the so-called tanker war of 1987. Hussein went so far as to employ chemical warfare against the Iranians. The war dragged on for eight long years, bringing misery, suffering, and death to both sides. Finally, a cease-fire went into effect in 1988. The Iraqi Army had been battle hardened by eight years of combat.

LEFT: The frigate USS *Stark* lists to port after being struck by an Iraqi Exocet missile on May 17, 1987, that killed 37. The next day, Iraq apologized for the attack, saying it was an accident.

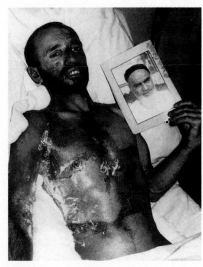

FAR LEFT: Iraqi troops in Faw, Iraq, stand in front of a bullet-riddled portrait of the Ayatollah Khomeini on April 21, 1988. The Iraqis earlier had retaken the Faw Peninsula during a 36-hour offensive.

LEFT: An Iranian soldier holds a portrait of Khomeini while being treated in a hospital in London. Iranian diplomats said the soldier's injuries were caused by Iraqi chemical weapons.

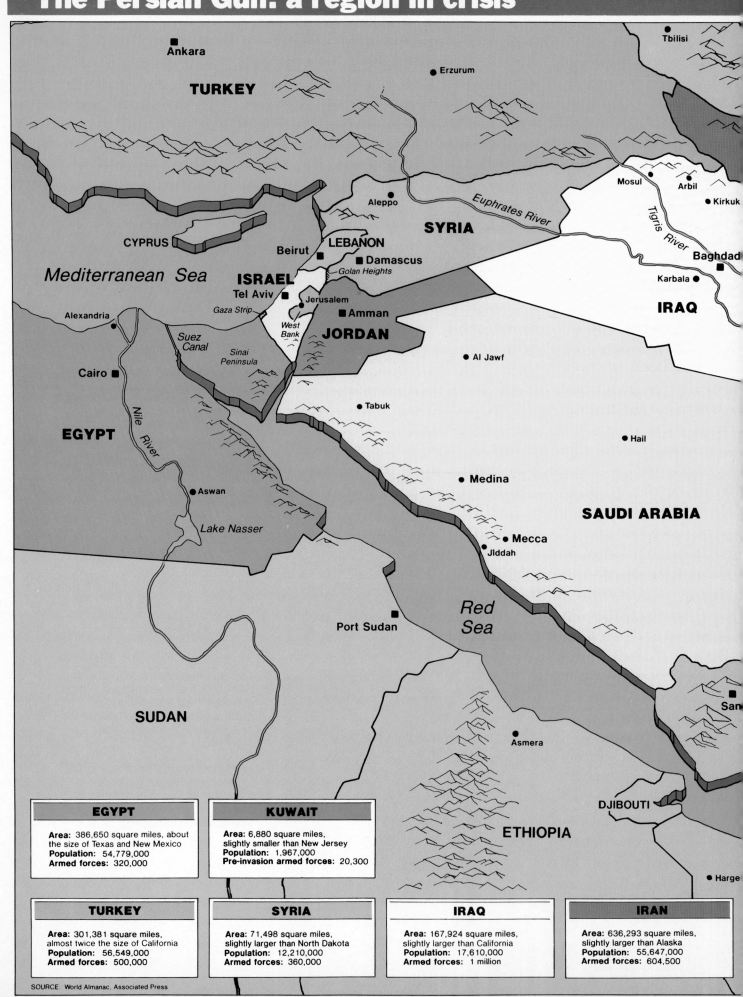

The Persian Gulf: a region in crisis

Tbilisi

Ankara

TURKEY

Erzurum

Mosul Arbil

Kirkuk

Aleppo

SYRIA

Euphrates River

Tigris River

Baghdad

CYPRUS

LEBANON

Beirut ■

Damascus

Mediterranean Sea

ISRAEL

Golan Heights

Karbala

Tel Aviv ■

Jerusalem ■

IRAQ

Gaza Strip

Amman ■

Alexandria

Suez Canal

West Bank

JORDAN

Al Jawf

Sinai Peninsula

Cairo ■

Tabuk

Hail

EGYPT

Nile River

Medina

Aswan

SAUDI ARABIA

Lake Nasser

Mecca

Jiddah

Red Sea

San

Port Sudan

SUDAN

Asmera

DJIBOUTI

ETHIOPIA

Harge

EGYPT

Area: 386,650 square miles, about the size of Texas and New Mexico
Population: 54,779,000
Armed forces: 320,000

KUWAIT

Area: 6,880 square miles, slightly smaller than New Jersey
Population: 1,967,000
Pre-invasion armed forces: 20,300

TURKEY

Area: 301,381 square miles, almost twice the size of California
Population: 56,549,000
Armed forces: 500,000

SYRIA

Area: 71,498 square miles, slightly larger than North Dakota
Population: 12,210,000
Armed forces: 360,000

IRAQ

Area: 167,924 square miles, slightly larger than California
Population: 17,610,000
Armed forces: 1 million

IRAN

Area: 636,293 square miles, slightly larger than Alaska
Population: 55,647,000
Armed forces: 604,500

SOURCE: World Almanac, Associated Press

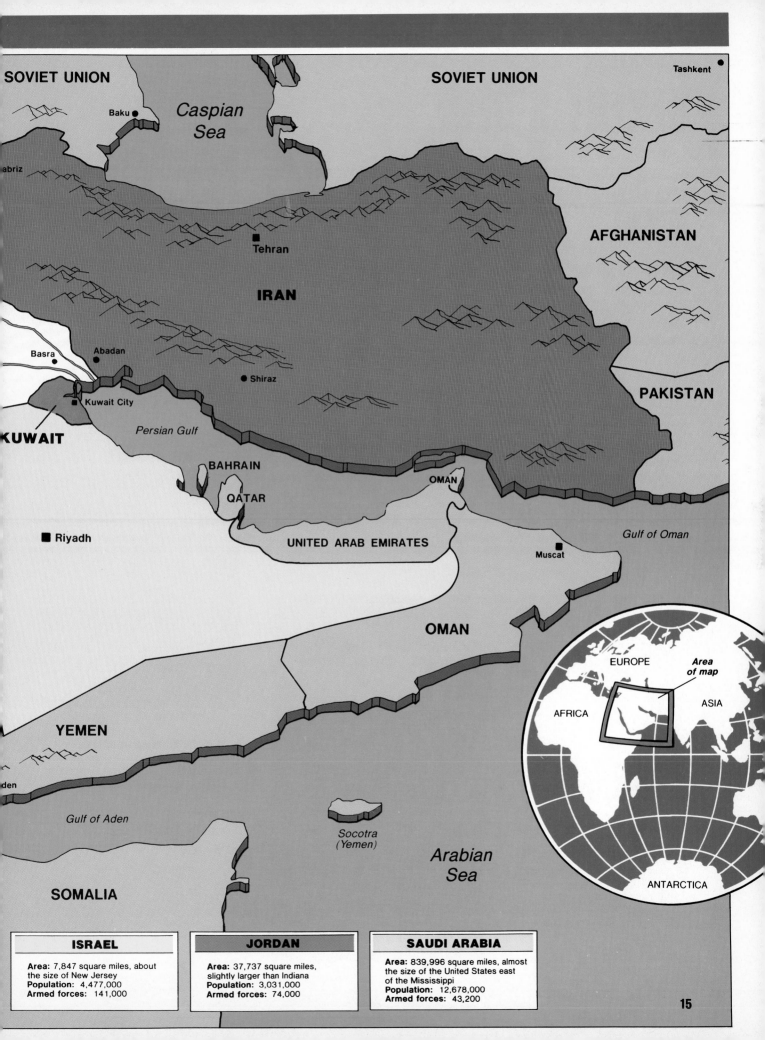

SOVIET UNION

Baku

Caspian Sea

SOVIET UNION

Tashkent

abriz

AFGHANISTAN

Tehran

IRAN

PAKISTAN

Basra

Abadan

Shiraz

Kuwait City

KUWAIT

Persian Gulf

BAHRAIN

QATAR

OMAN

Gulf of Oman

Riyadh

UNITED ARAB EMIRATES

Muscat

OMAN

YEMEN

den

Gulf of Aden

Socotra (Yemen)

Arabian Sea

SOMALIA

EUROPE

Area of map

AFRICA

ASIA

ANTARCTICA

ISRAEL
Area: 7,847 square miles, about the size of New Jersey **Population:** 4,477,000 **Armed forces:** 141,000

JORDAN
Area: 37,737 square miles, slightly larger than Indiana **Population:** 3,031,000 **Armed forces:** 74,000

SAUDI ARABIA
Area: 839,996 square miles, almost the size of the United States east of the Mississippi **Population:** 12,678,000 **Armed forces:** 43,200

OPERATION DESERT SHIELD

THE INVASION OF KUWAIT

After several weeks of saber rattling and tough talk, Saddam Hussein unleashed his battle-hardened army against Kuwait on August 2, 1990. The invasion caught much of the world by surprise: Many Middle East experts had thought that Hussein was only bluffing when his armies began massing on the Kuwaiti border prior to the outbreak of hostilities. In the event, Hussein's forces made short work of Kuwait; within the space of a few hours all organized resistance in that hapless country had ended, crushed beneath an Iraqi *blitzkrieg* of overwhelming strength and violence.

ABOVE: The emir of Kuwait, Sheik Jaber al-Ahmed al-Sabah, fled to Saudi Arabia by helicopter to avoid capture by invading Iraqi forces. Less fortunate was his younger brother Fahd, who was killed by Iraqi troops in the royal palace in Kuwait City.

LEFT: Under the watchful eye of a Jordanian policeman (right), two Kuwaiti refugees register at the Kuwaiti embassy in Amman on August 9, 1990.

ABOVE: These Kalashnikov-armed soldiers of the Iraqi Army, seen here in a pre-war parade in Baghdad, are outfitted in a motley of uniforms; their camouflage fatigues vary in style and color, one of them is wearing running shoes instead of combat boots, and at least two lack caps. Although unimpressive to look at, men such as these endured a bloody eight-year war with Iran, and swept through Kuwait in a matter of hours. LEFT: A few days after the fall of Kuwait, a Baghdad television station broadcast this image of an Iraqi armored personnel carrier and its crew purportedly leaving the country they had just conquered.

THE FAILURE OF DIPLOMACY

ABOVE: On January 9, 1991, Secretary of State James Baker (right) and Iraqi Foreign Minister Tariq Aziz met in Geneva, Switzerland, to discuss a possible resolution to the Gulf crisis. The two men are shown here shaking hands at the outset of their discussion, which ultimately yielded no change in the Iraqi position. RIGHT: While Iraq's President Saddam Hussein remained intransigent, his counterpart in the White House, President George Bush, pressed Congress to sanction the use of force against Iraq.

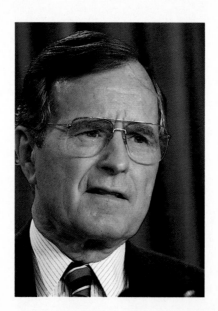

The world reacted with almost universal condemnation as Saddam Hussein announced that he would make Kuwait a graveyard if anyone attempted to stop him. In response, the General Assembly of the United Nations voted, without dissent, tough economic sanctions against Iraq—sanctions which all U.N. members were required to obey. President Bush and Secretary of State James Baker made continual diplomatic efforts to shore up the coalition against Iraq, a coalition made at once strong and fragile by Arab members like Egypt, Syria, and Morocco. The U.S. sought face-to-face talks with Hussein, and welcomed the efforts of other peacemakers, including President François Mitterrand of France, King Hussein of Jordan, and Secretary General of the United Nations Javier Perez de Cuellar. None of their efforts met with any success.

Arafat with Egypt's Hosni Mubarak.

Arafat with Libya's Muammar Qaddafi

Arafat with Saddam Hussein

ABOVE: In rebuffing all diplomatic overtures for a negotiated settlement, Saddam Hussein became more and more bellicose, demanding that any solution to the issue of Kuwait be linked to the Palestinian question. Yasser Arafat, the leader of the Palestine Liberation Organization, quickly seized upon this opportunity to further his cause. Many Arab leaders actively curried his favor, some exploited him for their own ends, while others merely tolerated him; none, however, could afford to ignore him and still remain popular with his own people.

ABOVE: On August 16, 1990, Jordan's King Hussein journeyed to President Bush's Kennebunkport, Maine, residence seeking ways to defuse the Gulf crisis. Shown here meeting with the press outside Bush's house, Hussein gives a resigned shrug that speaks volumes for the failure of his endeavor.

ABOVE: The diplomatic efforts of President Bush and Secretary of State James Baker seem to have made the correct impression upon France's President François Mitterrand. Failing in his efforts to make peace at the last moment by personal negotiations with Saddam Hussein, Mitterrand committed French Armed Forces to the coalition.

Americans bid farewell to each other as soldiers and sailors head off to war. OPPOSITE: A sailor fondly embraces his best girl. LEFT: A crewman on the aircraft carrier *Theodore Roosevelt* shares a last, quiet moment with his wife and baby daughter (top); a soldier reassures his daughter (middle); a simple but heartfelt sign says it all for this woman (bottom). ABOVE: A female soldier, and mother, holds hands with her daughter.

DESERT SHIELD BUILDUP

ABOVE: Marine Light Assault Vehicles arrive in Saudi Arabia in December 1990.

While diplomats negotiated, America and its allies continued the Desert Shield buildup at a furious pace. Years of training for such an eventuality now began to pay off as U.S. air, sea, and ground forces were dispatched to the Gulf region in ever-growing numbers. Not since World War II had the U.S. military undertaken an endeavor of this size and urgency. The first ground troops to arrive in Saudi Arabia found themselves in the furnace-like conditions of the Arabian desert facing a huge, combat-experienced Iraqi Army equipped with thousands of Soviet-built tanks and artillery pieces. Fortunately, the Allied coalition was protected by American Air Force and Navy warplanes, which patrolled the skies near the Kuwaiti border to deter Iraqi aggression — and not incidentally, to give the United Nations army the breathing space it needed to assemble its forces.

LEFT: American Bradley Infantry Fighting Vehicles form up in a long line after arriving in Saudi Arabia in August 1990.

DESERT SHIELD BUILDUP

ABOVE: The first of many U.S. Patriot missile batteries unloads from the cavernous interior of a C-5A transport plane. The Patriot would soon demonstrate that it was one of the most potent weapons in the American arsenal.

ABOVE: A gigantic M-1A1 Abrams Main Battle Tank, painted in desert camouflage colors, rumbles off the ramp of a tank landing ship onto a dock in Saudi Arabia. This 63-ton monster is quite possibly the most sophisticated and combat-capable tank ever built.

LEFT: After landing in Saudi Arabia in August 1990, troops of the 82nd Airborne Division emerge from the dark recesses of a C-5A transport into the bright desert sun. Midday temperatures during the first months of Operation Desert Shield often soared to 120 degrees, requiring soldiers to consume huge quantities of water to avoid dehydration and sunstroke. Enduring temperature extremes and inclement weather is something of a tradition for the 82nd Airborne Division: in the winter of 1944–45, this proud unit fought the German Army to a standstill in sub-zero conditions during the Battle of the Bulge.

HOME AWAY FROM HOME

ABOVE: The arrival of the first shipment of mail to American troops in Saudi Arabia is an occasion for good times and laughter.

It has been said that war is characterized by prolonged periods of unbearable boredom punctuated by moments of stark terror. Absent an Iraqi response, troops participating in Operation Desert Shield experienced very little of the latter and plenty of the former as they waited in the broiling Saudi desert for events to unfold on the diplomatic front. The sizzling summer heat precluded all but the most minimal activity during the day; consequently, military personnel spent a large measure of their free time reading and writing letters. Military leaders, aware that mail call in a foreign theater of war is a surefire morale-booster, made the delivery of mail to front-line troops a top priority. Of course, the troops weren't always reading and writing letters; at night, when the air cooled down, they underwent an intensive training program in preparation for the war with Iraq. The training schedule was grueling and tedious, but would serve the troops in good stead once the shooting began.

LEFT: Sitting in the meager shade of an armored vehicle, a soldier from the 24th Mechanized Infantry Division records impressions of his first day in Saudi Arabia.

ABOVE: Even in a time of impending war, the small chores of everyday life cannot be neglected. At his post in the Saudi desert, this American soldier is doing his laundry under a camouflage net beside his 155 millimeter self-propelled howitzer. Note the items hung out to dry above the folding cot. For a soldier in the field, cleanliness is as necessary as it is desirable; filthy clothing and encampments are breeders of disease, which was the chief cause of death in pre-modern armies. RIGHT: Compared to his billet in the United States, the American soldier shaving in the open air is laboring under fairly primitive conditions; however, compared to the lot endured by soldiers in past wars, he is living in the lap of luxury.

ABOVE: American troops involved in Operation Desert Shield quickly dubbed Saudi Arabia the Sandbox. The sand was everywhere, and seemed to get in everything, insidiously destroying electronics, engines, and even such seemingly invulnerable items like the barrels of cannons. Yet the desert environment wasn't always unpleasant; the trio of Marines pictured above have just taken advantage of one the few pleasures the Sandbox has to offer: a cooling dip in the Persian Gulf. This photograph was taken in October 1990, well before the outbreak of war; nevertheless, the Marines are well-armed with M16 rifles. LEFT: Morning finds one Marine undergoing a time-honored ritual of his service: the close-cropped haircut. The Marine Corps has always been a stickler about short hair, far more so than the Army.

Recreational activities became an important way to dispel tension and pass the time as the United Nations coalition geared up for war. OPPOSITE PAGE: Two American soldiers in the Saudi desert indulge in what is undoubtedly a merciless game of chess. CLOCKWISE FROM TOP LEFT: Soldiers from the 24th Mechanized Infantry Division catch up on the local news with the aid of an English-language Saudi newspaper; *The Forgotten Soldier,* an autobiographical account of a German soldier on the Russian front in World War II, provides relevant reading for this G.I.; cradling a walkie-talkie to his body, a soldier catches some shuteye during the midday heat in the shade of his Hummer (note the TOW antitank missile launcher on top of the vehicle); a pair of 82nd Airborne troopers take a load off their feet while their commanding officer talks on the radio; another group of 82nd Airborne troopers blow off steam with a fierce game of football.

ALLIED TROOPS IN THE UNITED NATIONS COALITION

King Fahd of Saudi Arabia.

The United Nations coalition that was mobilized against Iraq was truly international in scope. In addition to the United States and Canada, nations dispatching forces to the Gulf included a sizable European contingent (Britain, Italy, and France); the member states of the GCC, or Gulf Cooperation Council (Saudi Arabia, Bahrain, Qatar, and the United Arab Emirates); the Middle Eastern countries of Egypt, Syria, Turkey; and the Southwest Asian countries of Pakistan and Bangladesh. Forbidden by their respective constitutions from participating in military operations, both Germany and Japan have pledged significant financial assistance to the coalition, although it remains to be seen how much they actually contribute. Like all military alliances, the United Nations coalition is fragile and potentially fractious.

MAIN IMAGE: **These Saudi Arabian troops had the most to lose if Iraq was allowed to prevail in Kuwait.** INSET: **Saudi soldiers, intensely devoted to their faith, face the Islamic holy city of Mecca to perform their ritual daily prayers.**

Upon arriving in Saudi Arabia in September 1990, Egyptian Special Forces troops stand at attention in front of their American-built M-60 Main Battle Tanks.

Egypt's President Hosni Mubarak, seen here addressing the Egyptian Parliament in Cairo, has repeatedly shown himself to be a steadfast ally of the United States.

A French Mirage 2000 fighter. Initially restricted to hitting targets in Kuwait, the French Air Force soon broadened the scope of its activities to include Iraq.

Soldiers of the French Foreign Legion prepare to add a new chapter to that elite unit's long and proud tradition of desert warfare.

These soldiers of the United Arab Emirates are no doubt aware that their tiny, but immensely wealthy nations are likely candidates for Iraqi conquest.

Motivated by Iraq's notoriously brutal occupation of their homeland, soldiers of the Kuwaiti Volunteer Army train for combat with the hated forces of Saddam Hussein's army.

British troops man a gun emplacement in the Saudi desert. After the United States, Britain has contributed the most troops to the Gulf coalition.

Heavily armed British Royal Air Force Tornados, like the one pictured here, were used with great effectiveness in attacks on Iraqi airfields.

Italian troops, here shown in camouflage paint and their distinctive plumed helmets, represent an important European component of the U.N. coalition.

It is important to understand that, in terms of composition, the United Nations coalition in the Gulf is striving to achieve political as well as military objectives. The image of Arab, American, and European soldiers fighting side-by-side against a common foe—Saddam Hussein—is one intended to quash the subversive notion that the conflict is yet another instance of aggressive Western imperialism toward the nations and peoples of the Middle East. In particular, President Bush has expressed his hope that this unprecedented alliance will lead to the establishment of a new order in the region, one in which politically moderate states such as Egypt and Morocco hold sway over chronic troublemakers like Iraq.

Syrian women paratroopers parade in Damascus. As a member of the U.N. coalition, Syria could become a regional superpower in the event of an Iraqi defeat.

An infamously ruthless leader, Syria's President Hafez Al-Assad may be America's most unlikely partner in the Gulf coalition.

EAST MEETS WEST

U.S. soldiers stationed in the Mideast meet a lifestyle very different from anything they've known back home. Western life may include T.V., fast food, and movies. But electricity is not always available in the desert, and a nomad's idea of fun may have little to do with going to the movies. More significant differences involve religion and government. American soldiers are primarily Christian; their Arab hosts are very likely to be Muslims. The United States is a democracy, while most governments in the Mideast are not.

ABOVE: An M-1 Abrams tank rumbles through the Saudi Arabian desert behind a line of camels during Operation Desert Shield. LEFT: A Saudi man in traditional Middle East garb strolls past soldiers in fatigues working on an AH-64 Apache helicopter. Such contrasts are common in the Mideast. FAR LEFT: The Army MRE (Meal Ready to Eat) appears to hold the curiosity of, but little charm for, a Saudi bedouin who shares a meal with a U.S. soldier.

DESERT LIFE

LEFT: These soldiers of Company C, 8th Battalion, 2nd Marine Division pose after training exercises in northeast Saudi Arabia. They seem to be nonchalant about the camels so common to desert life. ABOVE, TOP: Water is vital in the desert; one soldier needs several gallons per day to survive. Desalination plants along the shore of the Persian Gulf provide much of that needed water. ABOVE, MIDDLE: Although most people think of the desert as hot, during the winter months temperatures can drop to freezing at night. Here, soldiers stand around a fire at dawn to keep warm. ABOVE, BOTTOM: An M-1A1 Abrams tank kicks up a cloud of sand while on patrol in the Saudi desert.

WOMEN IN THE U.S. ARMED FORCES

ABOVE: Women Marines present arms. Like all Marines, the women are trained to be proficient with firearms.

When Saudi Arabia's King Fahd made the decision to request Western intervention in the Gulf, he did so knowing that he would have to allow Western military personnel—men and, most especially, *women*—to operate from the sacred Arabian soil. Conservative and deeply religious, Saudi culture accordingly suffered an unbelievable shock. Women were supposed to wear clothes that covered them completely, yet American women soldiers—wearing fatigues and carrying the eternal symbol of Arab manhood, the rifle—were flooding in.

ABOVE: Air Force pilot Kim Rinta strides across the runway to the United Arab Emirates Hawk fight-bomber she is slated to fly. RIGHT: In her American-flag emblazoned flight suit, pilot Kim Rinta cuts a dashing figure in a land where women are obliged by religious and social strictures to maintain a low profile.

ABOVE: A woman technician replaces a vital electronic component.

ABOVE: Women operating heavy machinery is an unusual occurrence in a country where only men are permitted to drive.

CHEMICAL WARFARE: WEAPON OF DESPERATION

Chemical and biological warfare was first used during World War I. Protective equipment was of a primitive quality, and casualties were horrifying. Chemical weapons were not used in combat during World War II, although both sides possessed huge stockpiles of these deadly weapons. Today, about 15 nations possess chemical weapons, and at least eight nations—including Iraq—have used them within the past two decades.

Allied troops in the Mideast, as well as civilians, treated Saddam Hussein's threat to resort to chemical warfare seriously from the beginning; he used chemical weapons during the Iran-Iraq War. Armed forces and civilians must protect themselves against chemical weapons. Troops are equipped with gas masks and protective suits. Many civilians, especially in Israel, possess gas masks. In an ironic twist, Iraq's ability to produce the chemical weapons that now threaten Allied troops is partly owed to German firms that illegally sold Iraq the necessary technology.

OPPOSITE: In the U.S. military, protective clothing is standard issue and chemical warfare defensive training is routine. However, when temperatures start to soar in the desert, these suits can become extremely hot and uncomfortable, reducing fighting ability.
ABOVE: Two soldiers of the 3rd Marine Regiment, based in Hawaii, test a gas mask at an air base in Saudi Arabia.

LEFT: These Egyptian troops—members of the Allied coalition—wear gas masks as they step into formation for a training exercise with chemical warfare gear.

CHEMICAL WARFARE: WEAPON OF DESPERATION

ABOVE: When Saddam Hussein threatened to attack Israel with Scud missiles, it was not known if the missiles would be armed with chemical warheads. Thus, when the sirens sounded in Israel, Israeli citizens headed to sealed rooms and began to don gas masks. The danger of chemical weapons caused much fear and tension throughout Israel. RIGHT: For babies and small children, protective plastic tents become necessary because gas masks are too large.

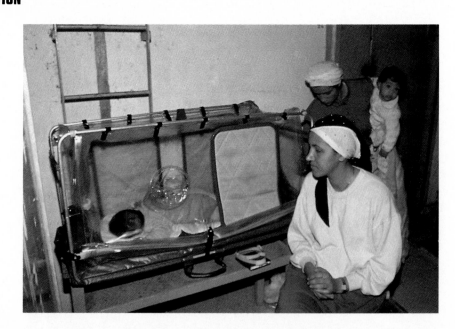

ABOVE: The terror of chemical weapons knows no bounds of Arab brotherhood. Hussein launched Scud missile attacks toward Dhahran, Saudi Arabia, forcing fellow Arabs to don gas masks for protection. LEFT: Waiters of the International Hotel in Dhahran sit out an air alert.

COMMANDER IN CHIEF IN THE FIELD

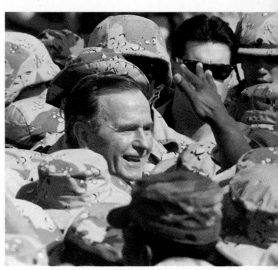

LEFT: President George Bush shares lunch with U.S. troops on November 22, 1990, during his Thanksgiving Day visit to Saudi Arabia. ABOVE, TOP: George and Barbara Bush wave goodbye to U.S. Marines as they prepare to leave the Mideast. ABOVE, BOTTOM: Over the Thanksgiving holiday, President Bush visited troops in the Mideast to boost morale and to gauge their mood.

COUNTDOWN TO DEADLINE

ABOVE: U.S. troops leave a few choice messages for Saddam Hussein on bombs destined for Iraq.

Diplomats struggled for a solution while the world watched in surprise and dismay. There seemed no avoiding the January 15, 1991, deadline set by the U.N. for Iraq to begin withdrawing from Kuwait. In the meantime, Operation Desert Shield continued its buildup. With the possibility of war looming ever closer, soldiers had to train, exercise, and prepare for all contingencies of battle. Training for desert warfare would be different from the usual preparation U.S. troops received for warfare in Europe. Still, many elements remained the same: Rifles needed to be cleaned, troops dug in—a time-honored infantry tradition, and target practice continued. Through it all, soldiers prepared for the possibility of chemical warfare. Protective suits are hot, and sweat builds up quickly. Visibility is hampered, and movement is difficult and awkward. Wearing protective chemical warfare clothing reduces combat efficiency by 30 to 50 percent.

LEFT: Tanks—such as these M-1 Abrams on patrol—play a significant role in any ground combat.

COUNTDOWN TO DEADLINE

LEFT: An A-6 Intruder prepares for takeoff from the aircraft carrier *Independence.* Aircraft flew patrol, reconnaissance, and training missions throughout the five months leading up to Operation Desert Storm.

RIGHT, TOP: Soldiers in Saudi Arabia had to deal with fine, windblown sand that got into every nook and cranny. Rifles and other equipment had to be cleaned constantly. RIGHT, MIDDLE: Troops of the 82nd Airborne Division stand at ease with their M16 rifles. RIGHT, BOTTOM: A U.S. Marine in Saudi Arabia trains for chemical warfare in December 1990.

LEFT: With their M16 rifles stacked, these soldiers begin the process of digging in. ABOVE: The digging in continues. No matter where infantry are stationed, trenches are necessary for protection. BELOW: Once the job is done, a trench can almost feel like "home." The trench may not be as comfortable, but at least it's safe. RIGHT: This soldier's face wears the look of the calm before the storm.

ABOVE: These American troops near the Kuwaiti border are well dug in. The young soldiers brought their rock 'n' roll, with a touch of humor, to this Islamic nation.

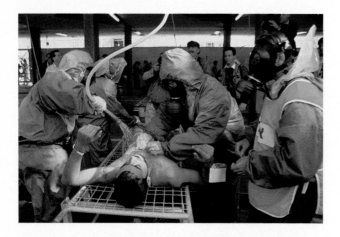

ABOVE: In any battle, there will be casualties. As fighting troops must train, so must medical personnel. In this case, they exercise for treatment of chemical warfare injuries. BELOW: Two soldiers diagram a plan of action in the sand.

ABOVE: The 82nd Airborne Division takes rifle target practice in Saudi Arabia in September 1990. RIGHT: As the January 15, 1991, deadline approached, infantry troops moved into position closer to the Iraq-Saudi and Kuwait-Saudi borders.

OPERATION DESERT STORM

THE FIRST BLOW: THE BOMBING OF BAGHDAD

ABOVE: **High-tech payoff: The view through a jet's camera of a smart-bomb target.**

The January 15, 1991, U.N. deadline came and went. Much of the world still hoped for a diplomatic solution. At three o'clock on the morning of January 17, 1991 (7:00 P.M., January 16, Washington, D.C., time), U.S. F-15E Eagles streaked across the night sky of Baghdad and a powerful, precise bombing raid began. Operation Desert Shield had become Operation Desert Storm. Cable News Network reporters brought the attack on Baghdad to the world as it was happening. All across Iraq, Allied forces ran sortie after sortie—more than 1,000 in the first 14 hours—determined to break the offensive capability of Iraq's war machine.

LEFT: **The night sky of Baghdad is lit up with tracers on the first night of Desert Storm.**

ABOVE: F-15E Strike Eagles were not the only Eagles to fly missions on the first night of Desert Storm. F-15 Eagle fighters, such as this one, also participated, providing air cover for other aircraft. RIGHT: Secretary of Defense Richard Cheney (left) and Chairman of the Joint Chiefs of Staff General Colin Powell (right) brief reporters at the Pentagon within the opening hours of Desert Storm.

ABOVE: The U.S. embassy in Baghdad a few months before the start of Desert Storm. RIGHT: Allied bombing of Baghdad continued into the dawn hours; tracers are visible on the far right. BELOW: The Iraqi Ministry of Defense in Baghdad burns just hours after U.S. and Allied bombs hit it on January 17, 1991.

A CLASH OF WILLS

RIGHT: Iraqi President Saddam Hussein —dressed in a military uniform— kneels in prayer. Hussein rules his Islamic country with an iron hand, allowing no dissent or opposition. Hussein claimed Kuwait was cheating on oil production, harming the Iraqi economy. Hussein also believed Iraq had an historical claim to Kuwait.
ABOVE: An Iraqi soldier kisses Hussein's hand in this TV image, which gives an indication of the personality cult of Hussein.

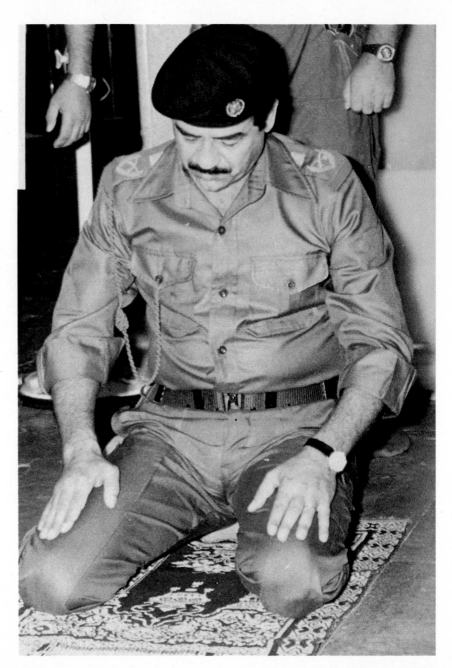

While Hussein and Bush square off with a war of words, a war of soldiers and machines takes place near Kuwait. HMMWVs (left) replaced the Jeep for U.S. armed forces. Saudi and American troops (center) work together to coordinate Allied fire power. An A-6 Intruder launches a Tomahawk missile (right). The Tomahawk cruise missile is so versatile it can be launched from aircraft, ships, or submarines.

LEFT: President of the United States George Bush—leader of the free world—believed Iraq's aggression toward Kuwait could not be allowed to go unpunished for fear that other dictators would feel free to act in the same manner. Also, Hussein's conquest of Kuwait threatened the oil fields of Saudi Arabia. Bush did not want a large portion of Middle Eastern oil reserves to fall under the control of one man, which would endanger the industrialized economies of the West. ABOVE: George Bush addressed the United States in his State of the Union speech on January 29, 1991. The State of the Union address represents the responsibility the President has toward the citizens who freely elected him.

The destroyer *Merrill* fires a Tomahawk (left). Sea-launched cruise missiles could be very effective against hardened Iraqi positions. One of the greatest fears Allied troops face is the danger of chemical warfare (center). From the beginning of Desert Storm, Hussein has attempted to draw Israel into the war by attacking that nation with Scud missiles (right), hoping to break apart the fragile coalition against Iraq.

SOLDIERS AND MACHINES

LEFT: General H. Norman Schwarzkopf—overall commander of Allied forces in the Mideast—chats with troops of the 354th Tactical Air Force Wing. Schwarzkopf said Allied troops would "kick [Hussein's] butt" should he cross the Saudi border.

FAR LEFT and LEFT: HMMWVs (Hummers) are versatile vehicles that provide mobility to ground troops. Hummers can also perform roles ranging from field car to TOW-carrying tank buster.

LEFT: Marines on maneuvers in late January 1991

RIGHT: Heavy artillery, such as the M109 Self-propelled Howitzer, provides major support for Allied troops who may be "Baghdad Bound."

THE WAR IN THE AIR

A mission for an F-15 Eagle starts with the pilot suiting up. The G-suit prevents the pilot from passing out when making high G maneuvers.

Once the pilot is in the aircraft, ground crew members go through an extensive checklist of the plane's systems.

Unlike other Eagles, the F-15E Eagle is a two-seater. The pilot and weapons operator must coordinate their actions for a successful mission.

After takeoff, the aircraft pilot hooks up with his wingman and any other support aircraft before heading toward the target.

The instrument panel of an F-15 Eagle. Although it may look complicated, the panel is actually easier to read than panels of the 1940s and 1950s.

Finally, with the help of innumerable support aircraft (such as Wild Weasels and AWACS), the target is reached, and it's bombs away.

ABOVE: A Kuwaiti A-4 jet fighter takes off from an airfield in Saudi Arabia for a combat mission against Iraqi forces.
LEFT: A member of a Saudi Arabian ground crew prepares an F-111 Aardvark for a mission.

ABOVE: The A-10 Thunderbolt II, more commonly known as the Warthog, is a tank killer of the highest ability. This tough aircraft is also heavily armored to withstand the rigors of close air support. RIGHT: The A-10's powerful GAU-8 Avenger 30mm rotary cannon is the centerpiece of the aircraft's armament.

LEFT: In the opening weeks of the Gulf War, B-52 Stratofortresses flew missions daily against Republican Guard forces dug in along the Iraq-Kuwait border. BELOW: A B-52 loads up on bombs; one Stratofortress can deliver up to 60,000 pounds of bombs.

THE WAR ON THE GROUND

ABOVE: The day before Desert Storm began, this convoy of military vehicles headed westward toward the Saudi-Kuwait border. BELOW: M-1 Abrams tanks were designed to meet and defeat the most advanced Soviet tanks in the event of war in Europe. Iraq possesses the same types of Soviet tanks. RIGHT: The job of the infantry is to take and hold ground, whether in Europe, Panama, or the Middle East. Tanks support that job.

ABOVE: Marines train with a 60mm mortar in late January 1991. BELOW: This British soldier is a part of the second largest Allied contingent in Saudi Arabia. RIGHT: A line of self-propelled howitzers moves toward the front after the outbreak of hostilities in the Mideast. OPPOSITE: The M198 155mm Towed Howitzer can throw a shell some 13 miles.

To protect its oil interests, the United States has maintained a naval presence in the Persian Gulf for years. As such, the U.S. Navy saw some of the earliest action in the Gulf. LEFT: *Iowa*-class battleships are equipped with huge 16-inch guns that can blast dug-in infantry positions. ABOVE: *Nimitz*-class aircraft carriers like the nuclear-powered *Eisenhower* provide a major air element to Operation Desert Storm. RIGHT: Tomahawk cruise missiles—capable of being launched from a range of platforms—gave new life to *Iowa*-class battleships. FAR RIGHT: The Tomahawk packs enough explosive to take out enemy positions that are too dangerous for manned attacks.

HUSSEIN STRIKES BACK

LEFT: Saddam Hussein's first response to Operation Desert Storm was to launch several Scud missile attacks at Israel and Saudi Arabia. Although most Scud missiles were shot down by Patriot missiles, one got through to Riyadh, Saudi Arabia, on January 25, 1991, killing one person. ABOVE: A petroleum storage tank near the Kuwait border burns after being hit by Iraqi shelling.

ABOVE: The night sky over Riyadh, Saudi Arabia, during an Iraqi Scud missile attack.

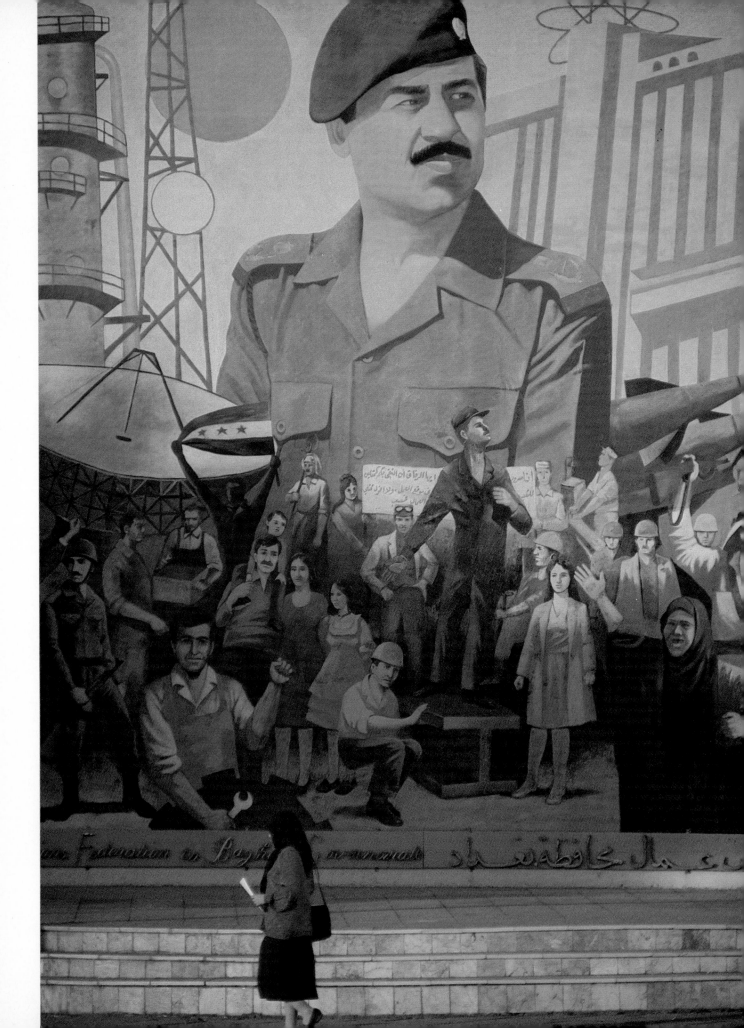

THE ENEMY: SADDAM HUSSEIN AND IRAQ

Saddam Hussein is widely regarded as one of the world's most ruthless leaders, and for good reason. Since assuming the role of Iraq's president and Commander in Chief in 1979, Hussein has never hesitated to ferociously suppress even the slightest murmur of opposition to his regime. In Iraq it is death for anyone, famous or humble, to say a single word against the "Father-Leader." Twelve days after his inauguration as president, for instance, he ordered the execution of 22 highly placed government officials, including members of the Revolutionary Command Council Cabinet and some of his closest personal friends. Reportedly, many were killed by his own hand.

LEFT: **In Iraq, the face of Saddam Hussein appears at every turn—in the media, on posters, in architecture and sculpture and even in the sky, as uncanny laser light shows pair his image with that of his hero, Nebuchadnezzar.**

ABOVE: **In September 1990—shortly after Iraq's conquest of Kuwait—these casually dressed American detainees were photographed beneath a typically enormous image of Saddam Hussein. The Americans, euphemistically called guests by Hussein (who had ordered them taken hostage), were later released unharmed.** LEFT: **A breadline in Baghdad, testimony to the fact that all is not well in Saddam Hussein's paradise.**

THE ENEMY: SADDAM HUSSEIN AND IRAQ

ABOVE: Iraq entered the war with about 30 Soviet MiG-29 Fulcrum fighters like the one pictured here.

ABOVE: The French-built F-1 Mirage fighter (shown here with Ecuadorian markings) was a mainstay of the Iraqi Air Force.

LEFT: Soldiers of Saddam Hussein's army pose in front of a poster glorifying their leader, as well as their own courage and heroism in the war with Iran. Iraq lost more than 120,000 men and spent more than 120 billion dollars during that ghastly eight-year conflict, which lasted from 1980 through 1988. Hussein now portrays the war with Iran as the self-sacrificing containment of crazed Iranian fundamentalists.

ABOVE, TOP: An Iraqi soldier takes aim with a Rifle Propelled Grenade (RPG) launcher, a rather outdated antitank weapon that is of little use against the thick armor of U.S. M-1 Abrams tanks. Hussein's somewhat antiquated war machine was far outclassed by the high-tech weaponry of the United Nations coalition. **ABOVE, MIDDLE:** A veteran Iraqi soldier introduces conscripts to the nuances of the AK-47 rifle in September 1990. Soldiers such as these, hastily mobilized to counter the threat of a U.N. invasion, were thrust into the front lines on the Saudi border in a cynical ploy to absorb the brunt of an Allied assault. **LEFT:** A woman soldier of the Iraqi Army shoulders a Kalashnikov automatic rifle.

ISRAEL UNDER ATTACK

ABOVE: **Having donned their gas masks, two Israeli girls wait out a Scud attack in a room sealed with plastic tape.**

Saddam Hussein has never deviated from an intense, almost hysterical hatred of Israel. Perhaps the most cynical expression of this was an assurance by Tariq Aziz, Iraq's foreign minister, who blithely told the world following his nation's invasion of Kuwait that Iraq would launch an unprovoked attack upon Israel if Iraq were confronted in the Gulf. Aziz was as good as Saddam Hussein's word; no sooner had Operation Desert Storm gotten underway than Scud missiles began pouring down on Israel. The first Scuds were launched against Israel in the predawn hours on Friday, January 18, 1991. Tel Aviv, Haifa, and Ramallah were hit by eight of the Iraqi missiles. Israel (and Saudi Arabia as well) would suffer many more Scud attacks in the days to come.

LEFT: **Gas masks at the ready, an Israeli family huddles together in their apartment during a Scud attack. The prospect that Hussein had armed his missiles with chemical warheads was an especial source of dread in these attacks.**

ISRAEL UNDER ATTACK

ABOVE: Israeli Prime Minister Yitzhak Shamir refused to rise to the bait that Saddam Hussein offered him through indiscriminate Scud attacks against the Jewish state. Aware that Hussein's deliberately provocative tactic was aimed at provoking an Israeli response, and thereby embroiling Israel in the Gulf War, Shamir chose not to retaliate—at least for the time being. Speaking for Shamir, Foreign Minister Benjamin Netanyahu explained the policy of restraint by saying, "We are going to act as the people of Israel expect us to act—with our heads, not with our hearts." LEFT: Israeli civilians in Tel Aviv inspect damage to their neighborhood after a January 23 Scud missile attack. The missile, which landed in a residential area, resulted in three deaths and over 70 injuries—all to civilians. Despite cries for vengeance, Shamir kept his military in check. Meanwhile, United Nations warplanes scoured the Iraqi hinterland in a determined effort to locate and destroy Hussein's elusive Scud missile launchers.

ABOVE: Anguished Israeli civilians contemplate their ruined homes, which have been leveled by a Scud missile. Shamir promised his countrymen that Israel would respond to Scud attacks in the place and time of its own choosing.

An apartment building in Tel Aviv burns after a Scud strike.

Israeli firemen hose down the smoking ruins of a building demolished in a Scud attack.

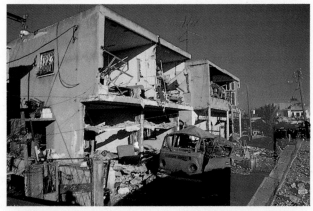

A Scud missile sheared off the outer wall of this Israeli apartment building, causing falling rubble to demolish a Volkswagen minibus.

One of the many civilian casualties of Scud attacks is lowered to a stretcher by her rescuers.

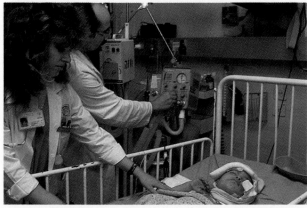

The victim of a Scud missile receives medical attention in the intensive care unit of an Israeli hospital.

A hospitalized casualty of a Scud attack is comforted.

LEFT: An Israeli father and his son sit in the rubble of their apartment building after a Scud attack. The Israeli populace reacted with angry stoicism to the missile barrage, taking comfort in Prime Minister Shamir's promise of eventual revenge against Iraq, as well as the realization that Hussein's days were numbered by Operation Desert Storm. The cardboard box at the man's side contains a gas mask.

PATRIOT MISSILE: SCUD BUSTER

From the very first day of Operation Desert Storm, it was evident that America's considerable investment in equipment and training had paid off. Perhaps the most crucial evidence, and certainly the most visually exciting, was the way in which U.S. Patriot tactical air-defense missiles countered Iraqi-launched Scud ballistic missiles. The thoroughly satisfying images of the Patriots reaching up through the mist to merge with the Scuds were matched in intensity by the pride on the faces of the troops operating the equipment, a pride that seemed to say, "By golly, it did work after all."

RIGHT: The Iraqi Al-Hussein (left) and Al-Abbas (right) missiles are longer-ranged variants of the Scud missile.

ABOVE: These Operator Tactics Trainer consoles are basically the same consoles used by Patriot missile system operators. The Patriot system is so versatile that it can simultaneously track and steer eight missiles to different targets. RIGHT: Each of these mobile Patriot launchers contains four missiles. Generally, at least two missiles are launched at each incoming Scud.

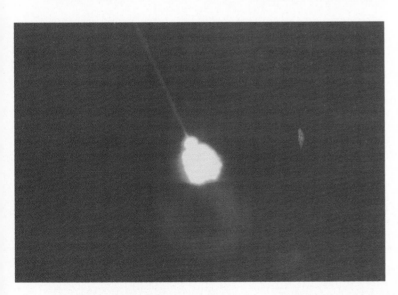

This photo sequence shows a Patriot missile test launching against a U.S. Lance Battlefield Support Missile. The final two photos show the Patriot missile intercepting and destroying the Lance in much the same fashion that it would destroy an Iraqi Scud missile.

The Patriot's first Scud kill was scored on January 18, 1991, at 4:28 A.M. in the skies over eastern Saudi Arabia. The use of the Patriot over urban areas in Israel occasionally resulted in civilian casualties and collateral damage to buildings from the falling

debris of destroyed Scuds. Nevertheless, Patriots managed to rack up a near-miraculous kill ratio against the Scuds, thereby earning the respect of the soldiers and civilians it was charged with defending.

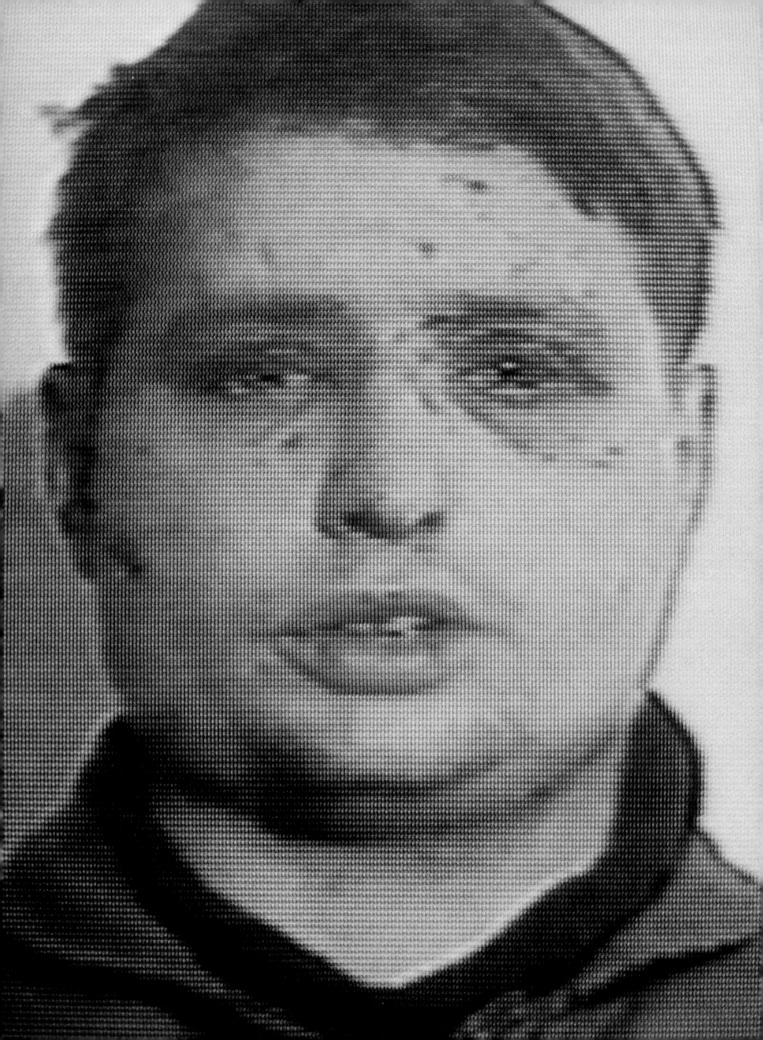

LEFT: **U.S. Navy Lieutenant Jeffrey N. Zaun, shown here on Iraqi television, displays cuts and facial bruises indicative of a severe beating. Speaking slowly and with a singular lack of emotion, Zaun condemned the war, saying, "I think our leaders and our people have wrongly attacked the peaceful people of Iraq." As he made these remarks, he glanced repeatedly to his right—perhaps to signal the presence of an armed guard stationed just off-camera to ensure Zaun's obedient recital of a speech that had clearly been prepared for him.**

ABOVE, LEFT: **British Flight Lieutenant John Peters, shot down by the Iraqis and placed before a television camera, appeared to be the most badly injured of the Allied airmen. His obligatory anti-war statement was delivered in an unintelligible mumble, and he seemed dazed by shock and pain and verging on unconsciousness. ABOVE: By contrast Italian Captain Maurizio Cocciolone, possibly unharmed, projected an air of defiance.**

The first Allied prisoners of war were airmen captured after their planes were shot down over Iraq-held territory. In direct violation of the 1949 Geneva Convention, which established rules governing the treatment of war prisoners, the Iraqis paraded eight of their captives on a state-run television program. Once before the camera the Allied pilots, some of whom appeared to have been beaten by their captors, proceeded to denounce the war in flat voices, using phrasings that sounded suspiciously like the propagandistic rhetoric of Iraqi officialdom. For their part, the Allies treated Iraqi prisoners in strict accordance to the rules set down by the Geneva Convention.

LEFT, ABOVE: **A U.S. Marine talks to one of a dozen Iraqi soldiers taken prisoner on an oil-drilling platform off the coast of Kuwait on January 19, 1991. The Iraqis had been manning an antiaircraft gun on the platform. LEFT: A Marine searches one of the captured Iraqi soldiers.**

OIL: INSTRUMENT OF WAR

Oil is the lifeblood of the West. Crude oil supplies the fuel that runs the world's factories and vehicles. Every Western nation relies heavily on oil to keep its economy running smoothly. The discovery of oil in the Mideast forever changed that region's place in the world. Suddenly, the Middle East mattered.

Not surprisingly, oil has played a military role during Operation Desert Storm. Allied planes attacked Iraqi refineries, hoping to cut the fuel production needed to run Iraq's war machine. Iraq created the world's largest oil spill, causing great harm to the Gulf's environment and threatening the desalination plants of Saudi Arabia.

ABOVE, TOP: **An oil refinery near Khafji, Saudi Arabia, burns from shelling as U.S. soldiers observe from a distance.** ABOVE, BOTTOM: **Sea Island Terminal just offshore of Kuwait — the source of the world's largest oil spill — burns after a gun battle between Allied and Iraqi ships.** RIGHT: **The oil spill caused by Saddam Hussein was an unmitigated ecological disaster. It may be years before the Persian Gulf recovers fully from the spill.**

REFUGEES: WAR'S FORGOTTEN VICTIMS

ABOVE: **Waiting is a common thread in refugee camps.** RIGHT: **A pregnant woman has all her belongings packed in a few suitcases. Depending on the length of the war, her child could be born in a refugee camp.**

As the unrelenting bombing of Iraq by Allied forces continued, life became more difficult in Iraq. Thousands of foreign nationals— from Africa, from Asia, from other Mideast nations—streamed across the Iraq-Jordan border. These refugees put enormous economic and humanitarian strains on Jordan. Life in a refugee camp is filled with hardships—crowding, poor shelter, shortages of basic items. Every war has its refugees; this does not make the suffering any less.

ABOVE, LEFT: **A refugee tries to maintain the routines of normal life.** ABOVE, RIGHT: **Refugees await a place to temporarily settle down.**

PEOPLE SPEAK OUT

As tensions mounted and then broke into Desert Storm, people around the world voiced their feelings about the Gulf War. Some favored military action, others protested against it. Palestinians supported Hussein, Kuwaitis opposed him. In all cases, passions ran high.

ABOVE and BELOW: **Palestinians in Amman, Jordan, demonstrate in support of Saddam Hussein, who has linked the Palestinian question with his withdrawal from Kuwait.**

ABOVE: **In London, a protester against the Gulf War expresses a common sentiment.** BELOW: **In January 1991, thousands of demonstrators opposing the Gulf War descended on Washington, D.C.**

ABOVE: A scene from a rally on Boston Common supporting U.S. troops in Saudi Arabia.

ABOVE: While one demonstration in Washington, D.C., opposed the Gulf War, another demonstration supported the action wholeheartedly. LEFT: Several thousand Kuwaiti citizens gathered in Abu Dhabi to demonstrate against Hussein's conquest of their nation.

America at the ready
—a U.S. soldier
in Saudi Arabia.

LAST MINUTE NEGOTIATIONS

CLOCKWISE FROM TOP LEFT: **Soviet Foreign Minister Alexander Bessmertnykh. Soviet special envoy Yevgeny Primakov. Mikhail Gorbachev meets with Tariq Aziz in Moscow.**

As Allied forces continued preparations for a ground war, the Soviet Union made a last attempt to find a peaceful solution. Soviet special envoy Yevgeny Primakov traveled to Baghdad to speak with Saddam Hussein. Iraqi Foreign Minister Tariq Aziz then went to Moscow to continue the talks with Soviet leader Mikhail Gorbachev and Soviet Foreign Minister Alexander Bessmertnykh. Since his safety while in the air over Iraq was not guaranteed by the Allies, Aziz was forced to travel by land to the Iranian border. He then caught a plane to Tehran; from there, Aziz flew to Moscow. The peace proposal fashioned by the Soviet Union and Iraq was filled with conditions that proved unacceptable to the Allied coalition. When George Bush set a deadline for an unconditional Iraqi withdrawal from Kuwait, a ground war became almost inevitable.

RIGHT: **Despite constant Allied air strikes, Saddam Hussein remained intransigent.** FAR RIGHT: **George Bush used the Allied military advantage to push for Iraq's complete compliance with all U.N. resolutions concerning the Gulf Crisis.**

THE GROUND CAMPAIGN

BATTLE FOR KHAFJI

ABOVE: Saudi and Qatari soldiers patrol the streets of Khafji after retaking the town in a fierce battle.

The last frantic negotiations between Iraq and the Soviet Union were in hopes of preventing a ground war that could possibly cause thousands of casualties. The Battle for Khafji—fought at the end of January—had already given a taste of what such a ground war could be like. Iraqi troops had thrust several miles into Saudi Arabia to capture the deserted border town of Khafji. The purpose of the attack was unclear: Was it a probing action by the Iraqi Army or was it an attempt to draw Allied forces into a ground campaign before Allied forces were ready for such action? After several days of fierce combat, Qatari and Saudi troops, backed by U.S. Marines, retook the town.

RIGHT: Qatari troops in armored vehicles move into Khafji during the battle to recapture the town.

BATTLE FOR KHAFJI

Allied troops celebrate their victory after the Battle for Khafji.

LEFT: An Allied armored vehicle burns in the aftermath of the Allied counterattack to recapture Khafji from Iraqi forces.
ABOVE: U.S. Marines supported Saudi and Qatari troops in the action to retake Khafji. Two Marine reconnaissance squadrons were in the town when the Iraqis entered; they remained there—hidden—and provided invaluable information to Allied troops outside the town.

THE FINAL PHASE

ABOVE: French and American soldiers hitch a ride into Iraq on a truck hauling a howitzer. **RIGHT:** Miles of convoys of Allied troops and equipment rolled into Iraq at the start of the final phase of Operation Desert Storm.

George Bush set a deadline of 12 noon February 23, 1991 (Washington, D.C. time), for Saddam Hussein to begin an unconditional withdrawal from Kuwait. Bush pushed for a quick Iraqi withdrawal to force the Iraqi Army to leave most of its tanks and heavy artillery behind, thus decimating Iraq's offensive military capability. Hussein refused to withdraw unconditionally.

Just hours after the deadline passed, Allied forces under General H. Norman Schwarzkopf moved against Iraqi positions. While a Marine amphibious group lay off the Kuwaiti coast, Allied and American soldiers thrust deep into Kuwait, covering as much as 50 miles in the first day. Meanwhile, troops of the 7th Army Corps moved directly into Iraq west of Kuwait, and some 2,000 soldiers of the 101st Airborne were airlifted 50 miles into Iraq via helicopter. This large flanking maneuver was intended to cut off the Iraqi Army in Kuwait and southern Iraq from supplies, and to block a possible route of retreat.

MAIN IMAGE: On the first day of the ground campaign, Allied forces quickly set up positions to hit the Iraqi Army with heavy artillery. INSET: These Allied soldiers in southern Iraq prepare heavy artillery shells for loading into their howitzers.

THE FINAL PHASE

ABOVE: An Allied soldier takes up a position during fighting in Kuwait. Saddam Hussein's army took a beating in what the Iraqi leader had previously predicted would be the "mother of all battles." The superior technology of Allied equipment was certainly a factor in that outcome, but the outstanding training and discipline of Allied warriors proved to be the real difference.

FAR LEFT: French and American forces quickly moved into southern Iraq. Here, a rocket is fired at an Iraqi position to soften it up before ground troops move in. LEFT: Great Britain contributed a large force to the Allied coalition. These British soldiers—involved in the fighting in southern Iraq— perform reconnaissance duties from the protection of a foxhole.

MASSIVE SURRENDER

ABOVE: In a scene that became representative of the Iraqi Army's lack of resistance, a line of Iraqi prisoners trudge past a group of U.S. Marines.

LEFT: Soon after the ground campaign commenced, scores of thousands of Iraqi soldiers began to surrender. Often, there were so many prisoners that the Allied advance was slowed. Here, Saudi troops clear out an Iraqi bunker (lower right) in southern Kuwait. ABOVE: Heavy air strikes had pounded Iraqi positions and cut off supplies, leaving many Iraqi soldiers in a bedraggled state. When they surrendered to Allied troops, many Iraqi prisoners of war kissed their captors in joy, gratitude, and relief.

TWO KEY BATTLES

The Allied victory was not without some bitter fighting. Two major battles occurred shortly before the Gulf War ended. One took place outside Kuwait City near the city's airport, when U.S. Marines engaged Iraqi troops with artillery and tanks, destroying at least 100 Iraqi tanks. Another major battle raged in Iraq west of the city of Basra. There, Allied troops and armor tangled with armored units of Hussein's much-touted Republican Guard. In a classic example of a desert tank battle, some 800 Allied tanks and armored vehicles crushed 300 Iraqi tanks and vehicles.

ABOVE: This smoldering Iraqi tank in southern Iraq was hit by a TOW missile during fighting between Hussein's warriors and the U.S. Army's 82nd Airborne Division. FAR LEFT: Fierce fighting occurred in southern Iraq between Allied forces and Republican Guard units. Here, U.S. soldiers ride atop a Sheridan tank, passing a ruined Iraqi tank. LEFT: A convoy of Kuwaiti troops and vehicles heads north toward Kuwait City during the action to force Iraq out of Kuwait. After difficult fighting near the Kuwait City airport, the capital of Kuwait was liberated.

LIBERATED KUWAIT

Jubilant citizens of Kuwait City mob an American Special Forces soldier after the city was liberated from Iraqi occupation on February 27, 1991.

PHOTO CREDITS: AP/Wide World Photos: Front Cover (inset), Back Cover (inset), 6 (bottom right), 9, 10, 11, 12 (top right, top left), 13 (top, bottom right), 17 (bottom), 25 (bottom), 37, 43 (bottom), 39 (top right), 51 (top), 58 (bottom right), 60 (top left, bottom left), 61 (bottom middle), 62 (bottom), 63, 65 (top), 68–69, 75 (top), 111 (bottom); **Armee De L'Air/Dassault Aviation:** 34 (middle left); **Artin/Sygma:** 19 (top left); **Terry Ashe/Gamma-Liaison:** 97 (top left); **D. Aubert/Sygma:** 85 (top left); **Esaias Baitel/Gamma-Liaison:** 25 (top); **Gilles Bassignac/Gamma-Liaison:** 74 (left), 75 (bottom), 102–103, 104–105; **Michael Baytoff/Black Star:** Front Cover (inset), 94 (bottom), 95 (bottom right); **James R. Benson Jr./Arms Communications:** 58 (top); **Dennis Brack/Black Star:** 22, 23, 33 (bottom), 50; **British Aerospace Inc.:** 35 (top right); **Alain Buu/Black Star:** 34 (top right); **Camerapress/Globe Photos:** 107 (bottom); **Dennis Cameron/Rex USA:** 44 (top), 85 (top right); **Dennis Cook/AP/Wide World Photos:** 97 (bottom right); **Charles Crowell/Black Star:** 34 (bottom left); **Larry Downing/Woodfin Camp & Assoc., Inc.:** Back Cover (inset), 70 (top, bottom right); **Alexis Duclos/Gamma-Liaison:** 94 (middle right); **P. Durand/Sygma:** 48–49, 90–91, 100–101; **J. Alan Elliott/United States Navy:** Front Cover (inset), 72; **John Ficara/Woodfin Camp & Assoc., Inc.:** 18 (bottom left); **D. Finley/Sygma:** 21 (top left, middle left); **Rick Friedman/Black Star:** 95 (top); **Gamma-Liaison:** 90 (bottom left); **Dean Garner/Arms Communications:** 6 (top), 64 (top right, middle left, middle right); **George Hall/Woodfin Camp & Assoc., Inc.:** 64 (top); **Dirck Halstead/Gamma-Liaison:** 97 (top right); **Hartwell/Sygma:** 31 (bottom right); **Chip Hires/Gamma-Liaison:** 45, 52 (bottom left), 90 (top left); **D. Hudson/Sygma:** 34 (middle right); **Nils Jorgensen/Rex USA:** 94 (top left); **William Kavel/Sygma:** 8 (bottom left); **P. Kern/Sygma:** 83 (bottom right), 84, 85 (bottom left, bottom right); **Kulik Photo/DOD/MGA:** 64 (bottom left); **J.P. Laffont/Sygma:** 67 (bottom); **Jacques Langevin/Sygma:** Front Cover (left, inset), Back Cover (inset), 27, 31 (top right), 42, 52 (top left, bottom right), 53, 68 (bottom left), 86 (bottom right), 96; **Ph. Ledru/Sygma:** 8 (top right); **B. Markel/Gamma-Liaison:** 57, 88, 89; **Tannen Maury/AP/Wide World Photos:** 110–111; **Joe McKeown/Rex USA:** 7 (top); **Wally Mcnamee/Woodfin Camp & Assoc., Inc.:** 6 (bottom left); **Georges Merillon/Gamma-Liaison:** 98–99; **Sadayuki Mikami/AP/Wide World Photos:** 109 (top); **Moshe Milner/Sygma:** 44 (bottom), 54 (top), 61 (bottom right), 80–81, 82–83, 85 (middle left, middle right); **Christopher Morris/Black Star:** 4–5, 32–33, 34 (bottom left), 39 (bottom right), 51 (top), 70 (bottom left), 78, 79 (bottom); **Timothy A. Murphy:** 61 (top left, top right); **Alain Nogues/Sygma:** 16 (top), 33 (right); **M. Philippot/Sygma:** 19 (bottom right); **Photri:** Front Cover (inset), Back Cover (inset), 8 (bottom right), 30, 35 (middle left), 40 (top, middle, bottom left), 40–41, 52 (top right), 54 (middle), 60 (bottom right), 61 (bottom left), 62 (middle right), 65 (bottom), 67 (top), 73 (bottom left), 79 (middle right); **Noel Quidu/Gamma-Liaison:** 94 (top); **Laurent Rebours/AP/Wide World Photos:** 108–109, 112 (top); **Ken Regan/Camera Five:** 28 (bottom), 31 (middle left, bottom left), 51 (middle), 54–55, 77, 79 (middle right), 92, 93; **Reuters/Bettmann:** Front Cover (inset), Back Cover (inset), 13 (bottom left), 16 (bottom), 17 (top), 18 (top), 19 (top right), 24–25, 26–27, 28 (top), 29 (top), 31 (top left), 34 (top left), 35 (bottom left, bottom right), 36–37, 43 (top), 46–47, 59 (bottom middle), 60 (bottom middle), 62 (top), 79 (top right), 89, 95 (bottom right); **Rex USA:** 106–107 (top), 109 (bottom); **N. Schiller/AP/Wide World Photos:** 73 (top); **Mi Seitelman/Foto Consortium:** 64 (top left), 66 (bottom); **Linda Shaefer/Sygma:** 21 (right); **Shone/Gamma-Liaison:** 97 (middle); **Ch. Simonpietri/Sygma:** 8 (top left); **Tom Stoddart/Woodfin Camp & Assoc., Inc.:** 40 (bottom right); **Lee Stone/Sygma:** Back Cover (inset), 20, 21 (bottom left); **Anthony Suau/Black Star:** 49, 76; **Sygma:** 19 (top right), 56–57, 60 (top right), 97 (bottom right); **A. Tannenbaum/Sygma:** 83 (top right); **Peter Turnley/Black Star:** 29 (bottom), 38–39, 39 (middle right), 62 (middle left); **United States Department of Defense:** Front Cover (inset), 64 (bottom right), 73 (bottom right), 86 (top right), 86 (left), 87; **Official United States Navy Photo:** 12 (bottom); **United States Air Force:** 71, 79 (top left); **L. Van Der Stockt/Gamma-Liaison:** 59 (top right), 102, 106 (bottom); **Vienna Report/Sygma:** 18 (bottom right); **WSMR/United States Army:** 87 (bottom left, bottom right); **Zone Five/Arms Communications:** 7 (bottom)